YOU CAN

RICH
HOUGH

SAVE THE PLANET

A DAY IN THE LIFE OF YOUR CARBON FOOTPRINT

A & C Black • London

theguardian

Published 2007 by A & C Black
Publishers Limited
38 Soho Square, London, W1D 3HB
www.acblack.com

ISBN 978-0-7136-8688-3

Copyright text © The Guardian, 2007

Created by Bookwork Ltd, Stroud, UK

A CIP catalogue record for this book
is available from the British Library.

A & C Black uses paper produced
with elemental chlorine-free pulp,
harvested from managed sustainable
forests. It is natural, renewable and
recyclable. The logging and
manufacturing processes conform
to the environmental regulations of
the country of origin.

Printed and bound in Milan by Rotolito on
100% recycled paper.

All the Internet addresses given in this
book were correct at the time of going to
press. The author and publishers regret
any inconvenience caused if addresses
have changed or sites have ceased to
exist, but can accept no responsibility for
any such changes.

SAVING THE PLANET

When I was a child, back in the seventies, my friends and I were convinced that civilization was about to be wiped out by nuclear war. It wasn't just an idle fear; everyone felt that way during the Cold War as the USA and Soviet Union competed to build nuclear weapons, and made threatening noises. There didn't seem much I could do in the way of ending the arms race, but I read books about radiation sickness, imagined all my hair and teeth falling out and worried how food could be grown in earth that had been poisoned.

In the end the superpowers made a grumpy sort of peace. It's nice to think that my own children are not anxious about nuclear war, but they have something else to worry about. Humans are threatening to destroy the planet in a different way.

Ever since the Industrial Revolution, 200 years ago, people have been living in a way that puts pressure on Earth's natural resources. All those years we were campaigning against nuclear bombs, we were developing more bad habits: driving everywhere, flying more often, using stacks of plastic bags and leaving lights on everywhere we went. The planet, after years of neglect and thoughtlessness, is in a bad way as a result. New dangers are springing up like acne.

The good news is that there are things we can all do, every day, which will really make a difference. From changing your own bad habits to getting your friends and family involved, this book will give you loads of ideas for saving the planet.

Best of all, it will give you the information you need to start campaigning: write letters to politicians and business leaders, ask teachers and school leaders what your school is doing about climate change, and nag your family as much as they nag you. Because one person can make a difference. And that person could be you.

Bibi van der Zee

Bibi van der Zee writes about ethical living and the environment for the *Guardian*.

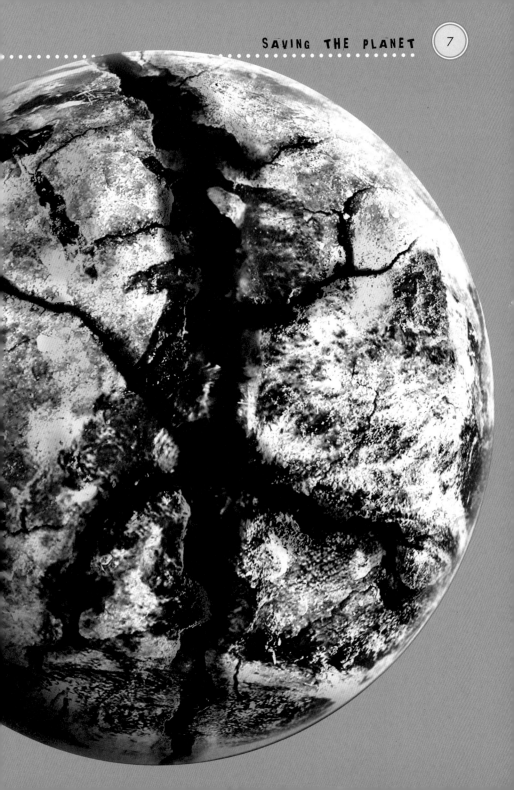

SCHOOL DAYS

We are all responsible for saving our planet. Even the smallest actions can make a real difference.

This section is packed with ideas for helping the planet on a school day. You will find out how to save water and energy. You will learn what Fairtrade is all about (see page 56) and will discover how to reduce your carbon footprint (see page 73).

EVERY DAY COUNTS
Each page looks at one part of a typical school day, from getting up in the morning and making your way to lessons, to relaxing in the evening and going to bed. On each left-hand page you'll find out about everyday things that harm the planet and its wildlife. On each right-hand page you'll find a list of practical steps that you can take to reduce your impact – starting today!

Use the diary at the end of the book to record your planet-saving actions.

GET EVERYONE INVOLVED
You can start using some of the ideas in this book right now. You will need help from your family or school staff to implement others, such as buying organic food and recycling paper. Some suggestions are for you to pass on to other members of your family. Remind them they are helping to save the planet. Try to persuade everyone – politely – to give up environmentally unfriendly habits, with this book to back you up! The planet is in serious trouble and your actions really will make a difference.

6.30 a.m.

CENTRAL HEATING

Central heating in the average household produces **3.6 tonnes** of carbon dioxide every year. That's enough to fill more than 200,000 party balloons.

EVERY DAY COUNTS...

Many households could reduce their carbon dioxide emissions by two tonnes per year by making their homes energy efficient. You can start helping in your home today.

Domestic carbon dioxide emissions have an enormous impact on the environment. Up to a quarter of all carbon dioxide emissions come from the fuels we use in our homes. Not only are most central heating systems inefficient, we burn huge amounts of gas to heat poorly insulated homes.

Of the heat energy produced in your home, as much as 33 per cent will be lost through the walls. Another third is lost through the roof and about 20 per cent is lost through drafty windows, doors and floorboards. This is not only a waste of energy but also a waste of money!

Most families tend to over-heat their homes instead of using 'personal insulation' such as heavy duvets and warm clothing. And hot water doesn't have to be scorching when it comes out of the tap. You have to mix it with cold water anyway. Lower temperatures mean fewer carbon dioxide emissions.

If the radiators in your home have their own thermostats, you can turn the temperature down in rooms you are not using.

Wear a sweater indoors and use a thick duvet or extra blanket on your bed. This means you can turn down the central heating in your bedroom and still be warm enough. **Draw the curtains** at dusk and move furniture away from the radiators to be more energy efficient.

Help to **stop hot air from escaping** by filling the gaps between floorboards and draught-proofing windows and doors. Find out if your hot water tank has a good **insulating jacket** and, if not, try to persuade your parents to get one. It will keep the water hot for longer. Insulation in the loft will trap hot air in a house.

Tell the person in charge of the thermostat on your boiler that a **setting of just 60°C** should be high enough for all your hot water needs. If your boiler needs replacing, suggest that your family has a high-efficiency, **condensing model** with programmable heating controls.

THE GREENHOUSE EFFECT AND GLOBAL WARMING

We need the greenhouse effect. Without it, the planet would be too cold for us to survive. But pollution is making the effect more powerful. This is the likely cause of global warming.

The Earth has an atmosphere – a layer of gases which surround the planet. Sunlight travels through the atmosphere and warms the Earth. The Earth then radiates energy to cool down. Some of this energy is trapped close to the Earth's surface by gases in the atmosphere. These gases include methane, water vapour and carbon dioxide. This is the greenhouse effect. It is responsible for making the Earth much warmer than it would otherwise be, so far from the Sun.

GLOBAL WARMING

Global temperatures go up and down naturally as a result of changes in the

Glaciers are melting. This will cause sea levels to rise and flood low-lying coastal areas and islands around the globe.

Polar bears need Arctic ice floes to catch their food. As the ice disappears, many are starving.

Sun's output and volcanic activity. Since the 19th century, however, the average surface temperature of the planet has increased by about 0.6°C. Most scientists think this rapid rise is due to an enhanced greenhouse effect. Deforestation and the burning of carbon-rich fossil fuels (coal, oil and gas) have increased the carbon dioxide in the atmosphere and therefore the power of the greenhouse effect.

THE FORECAST

How our climate will change is difficult to forecast precisely. Climatologists (scientists who study the weather) estimate a further global temperature increase of from 1.4°C to 5.8°C within the next 50 years. This global warming is predicted to have huge consequences for life on Earth. Some places will have more rain; other places will become drier. Most areas will become warmer and there may be many storms, floods and droughts in different parts of the world. Plants and animals all over the world will be affected as their habitats get warmer and change. For example, in the Arctic, the polar bear is already struggling to survive because its habitat is melting. It is now listed as a threatened species.

7.00 a.m.

IN THE BATHROOM

Two-thirds of the water used in our homes is used in the bathroom, with about 50 litres used per person for personal washing every day. 50 litres should be enough for all our daily water needs.

EVERY DAY COUNTS...

Your morning shower or bath will wash away many litres of water contaminated by grease, grime and – if you use shampoo or shower gel – hundreds of synthetic chemicals.

A bath of average depth demands at least 80 litres of water. A power shower can use just as much water in less than five minutes. Even a standard shower uses 35 litres in five minutes, which would fill about seven buckets.

Across the world, there are 12,000 cubic kilometres of polluted fresh water. That's enough to fill the ten largest river basins. Fifty per cent of our major rivers are seriously polluted or depleted.

Stand under a standard shower and **keep washing time to a minimum**. If you like the energetic jet of a power shower, your family could get a water-saver showerhead fitted. This feels like a power shower but uses around half the water.

Every year, European cosmetics manufacturers test their products on 38,000 animals. From 2009, the testing of cosmetic products and ingredients on animals will be banned throughout the European Union (EU), although a complete ban on the sale of products tested on animals will not come into effect until 2013.

More than 1000 chemicals currently used by manufacturers of cosmetics and toiletries are thought to harm living organisms. Some of these chemicals are strong enough to survive the journey through sewage treatment works into the sea.

About five billion items of 'essential personal hygiene products' (deodorants, shampoos, toothpaste and sunscreen) are sold annually. This means that five billion cans, bottles and plastic tubes are manufactured, emptied and thrown away every year.

Try to **use natural, organic** toiletries and cosmetics. But be warned: labels can be misleading so check them carefully. Look for the logo of an organic certification organization such as the Soil Association in the UK, or the United States Department of Agriculture (USDA) to **guarantee organic contents**.

Avoid buying over-packaged bathroom products and **recycle empty containers** where you can (see page 145).

Our demand for water has doubled over the last 30 years. Now the world is running out of water. By the year 2025, two-thirds of the world's population will face a water shortage.

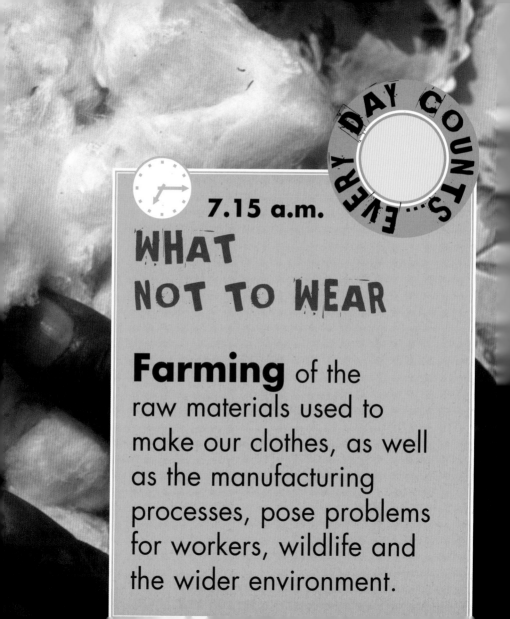

7.15 a.m.

WHAT NOT TO WEAR

Farming of the raw materials used to make our clothes, as well as the manufacturing processes, pose problems for workers, wildlife and the wider environment.

EVERY DAY COUNTS

Synthetic fibres have a huge impact on the environment, but natural fibres are a problem too. Cotton is the world's most polluting crop.

Almost 50 per cent of the textiles we buy are made from cotton. However, cotton farming can be a dangerous business. Ten per cent of all agricultural pesticides are applied to cotton crops. These chemicals pollute water supplies and can attack other organisms as well as pests. Pesticides poison three million people every year; 250,000 die as a result.

Many of the clothes sold in the West are imported – often from countries without laws to control working conditions. Employees, working in poor conditions, receive as little as 0.5 per cent of the price the clothes are sold for. This is well below the wage necessary for them to meet their food, shelter and health-care needs.

Many poor countries need to grow cotton to sell, on land that could be used for food crops.

Most synthetic fabrics are non-biodegradable. This means they do not get broken down by bacteria and decompose naturally. Nylon production also contributes to global warming with the release of the greenhouse gas nitrous oxide.

You won't be contributing to any of these problems – and you'll save energy – when you **buy second-hand** or 'vintage' garments. **Swap clothes** with your friends and if you're feeling creative recycle old or worn outfits into attractive, original designs.

 If you prefer to buy your clothes new, look for clothing made from organic textiles (including organic cotton and hemp) and **avoid synthetic fibres**.

Use the Internet to find a school uniform that is **made from organic cotton** and produced according to Fairtrade principles (see page 56). You can even buy **Fairtrade trainers**. Or buy second-hand. If your school does not sell second-hand uniforms, try looking at websites where you can buy and sell uniforms.

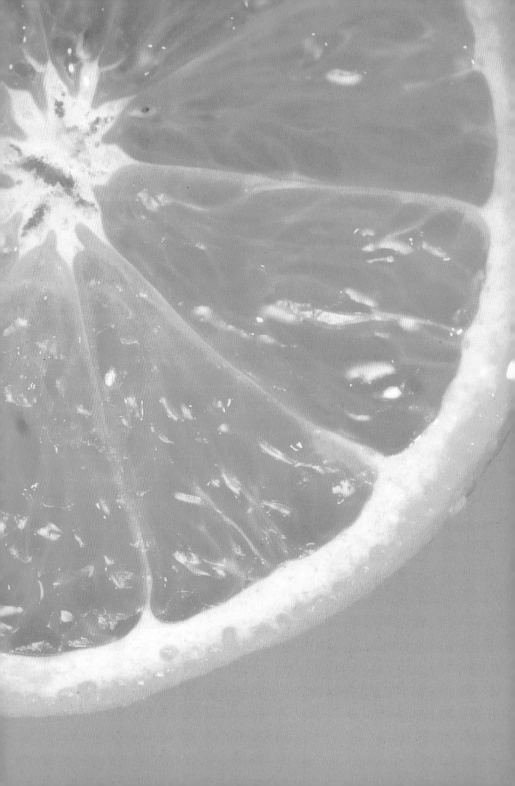

EVERY DAY COUNTS... COUNTS

7.30 a.m.

THE MOST IMPORTANT MEAL

To produce one glass of Brazilian orange juice, it is estimated that **22 glasses** of water are used in processing.

Before you sit down to eat breakfast, think about the impact your eggs, milky tea and orange juice have on the environment and on farm animals.

Battery-hens are kept indoors and never see daylight. They can be made to lay their eggs in cages narrower than an A4 sheet of paper. Their plight is of particular concern to the Compassion in World Farming Trust (CIWF). Although the EU had agreed to ban battery cages in 2012, the ruling is under threat from the farming industry – which has called for a further ten-year delay on the ban.

Ask your family to **buy eggs that are certified organic**. But don't trust every label you read. The number of hens permitted per hectare, and the definition of 'free-range' varies between organic certification organizations. The best place to get eggs is your local farmers' market so you know where they come from.

Hens that are truly free range are allowed to move around naturally outdoors.

EVERY DAY COUNTS...

Intensively farmed dairy cows suffer cramped and dirty conditions, making them prone to lameness and infection. Many dairy herds are given antibiotics daily to treat or prevent disease. This widespread use of antibiotics leads to the evolution of antibiotic-resistant bacteria, with serious consequences for human health.

The largest producer of orange juice is Brazil. It produces even more than Florida in the USA. In Europe, where Spain and Italy are major orange growers, 80 per cent of the orange juice consumed is imported from Brazil, massively increasing the energy expenditure and the food miles (see page 108) associated with the morning glass of 'OJ'. All those empty juice cartons are difficult to recycle and likely to end up as landfill.

To cut down on packaging – and trips to the supermarket – get milk and juice in **reusable bottles** delivered straight to your front door by your local dairy. Why not buy organic cereals, fruit and nuts in bulk to **create your own** healthy breakfast muesli?

When shopping for breakfast, it isn't difficult to **buy Fairtrade** and in many cases local organic produce. The Fairtrade Foundation supports a range of coffees, teas and fruit juices. You can get **organic meat, bread and dairy products** from most supermarkets.

ORGANIC FARMING

The large-scale, intensive farming of animals and food and textile crops has a harmful effect on the environment.

Modern farming practices involve the use of artificial chemical fertilizers and pesticides, which leak into waterways where they cause the rapid growth of algae, known as 'algal blooms'. The algae suffocate plants and animals that live in the water, killing lakes, rivers and other bodies of water. Pesticides can randomly destroy wildlife beyond their target pests and are often just as poisonous to the farmers that use them.

GENETICALLY MODIFIED (GM) CROPS

Crops may be genetically altered to make them hardier or less susceptible to disease. It is possible that ordinary varieties of the crops can become altered through cross-pollination. The long-term effect that GM crops could have on the health of people who eat them is still unknown.

THE IFOAM

Members of the International Federation of Organic Agriculture Movements (IFOAM) avoid the use of genetically modified crops, chemical fertilizers, pesticides, animal drugs and food additives. Instead, they use traditional farming techniques to work sustainably with the environment.

ORGANIC PRINCIPLES

Organic farming is based on natural ecological processes. It follows four principles – health, ecology, fairness and care. The principles relate to the environment as well as to all living things, from tiny organisms in the soil to human beings. When the principles are strictly followed, everyone involved in farming

Organic methods of pest control include using crop rotation and natural predators to prevent a build up of large populations of pests, such as caterpillars.

has a good quality of life, animals are kept in conditions that are as natural as possible for them, and there is less pollution. Those who produce, process, trade or consume organic products are helping to protect landscapes, climate, habitats, biodiversity, air and water.

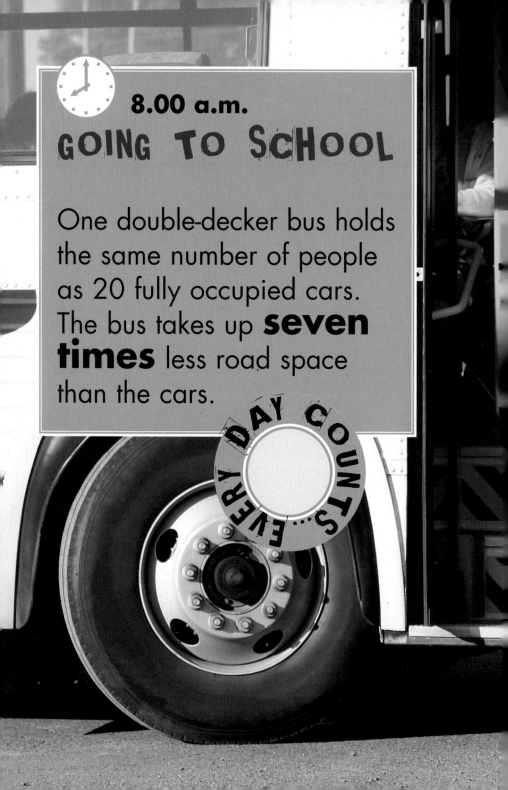

8.00 a.m.

GOING TO SCHOOL

One double-decker bus holds the same number of people as 20 fully occupied cars. The bus takes up **seven times** less road space than the cars.

EVERY DAY COUNTS...

There are more than 400 million cars and light trucks on the world's roads today. These vehicles are responsible for producing a huge amount of greenhouse gas. And this is not the only problem associated with road traffic.

Congestion is a problem in urban areas across the industrialized world. It leads to ground-level pollution. In the UK alone, 24,000 deaths are caused by poor air quality every year. We are becoming increasingly reliant on our cars. Twenty-two per cent of secondary school pupils and 41 per cent of primary school children are driven to school every day.

Each litre of petrol used in a car produces about 2 kilograms of carbon dioxide. It is estimated that at the current rate of population growth, together with economic growth, the total number of motor vehicles worldwide could rise to more than one billion by the year 2020. These vehicles would discharge as much as 1,800 million tonnes of carbon dioxide into the atmosphere in a year.

The recent trend for driving off-road vehicles in cities is often criticized. Sport Utility Vehicles (SUVs) use up to twice as much fuel as regular cars, causing three times the amount of atmospheric pollution.

If you get driven to school, help to set up a school run **rota system** for parents of pupils who live nearby. The more people who go in one car, the fewer cars there are on the road. Or go by bus. Better still, **cycle or walk** to school.

Give the drivers in your family a lesson on how to drive. They can **save fuel** by driving smoothly and efficiently – that is, not accelerating or braking too harshly, and **switching off the engine** when they are going to be stationary for a while. Air-conditioning burns fuel so use it only when necessary. Any extra load increases fuel consumption so **remove unused roof racks** and empty the junk from the boot.

If you know that someone is going to buy a new car, tell them to consider buying a **lower-emission car** or one that runs on cleaner, alternative fuels.

SAVE YOUR PLANET...

Vegetable oils can be turned into biodiesel, and bioethanol can be distilled from corn. Cars could run on these 'alternative' fuels.

12.30 p.m.

PACKED LUNCH

80 million food and drink cans end up in landfill every day in the UK – that's almost one and a half cans per person. Each person could fill a bath with the contents of their cans in a year.

EVERY DAY COUNTS...

Fast-food boxes, sweet wrappers and snack packets are our fastest-growing litter problem. Discarded fast food is a snack for rats. It has helped to swell the world rat population by millions.

Fast food is becoming increasingly popular, and millions of us drop litter, despite the threat of prosecution. It's no wonder that we have a problem with rubbish. As well as looking horrible, litter impacts further on the environment when it is eventually dumped in landfills or incinerated.

Fast food outlets clock up millions of food miles (see page 108). Even sandwich ingredients may have travelled around the world.

Instead of buying a pre-packaged sandwich, **make your own**. Not only can you control exactly what goes into it, but you'll cut down on excess packaging. If you buy food that has been produced locally, you will help to reduce the need for long-distance food transport and ultimately **save energy**.

SAVE YOUR PLANET...

More than half of the waste plastic generated every year is from packaging. This includes crisp packets, sandwich cartons and the billions of carrier bags given away by supermarkets. Non-biodegradable plastics cause environmental damage throughout their long lives.

Every year some 45,000 tonnes of plastic waste, including six-pack plastic rings, sandwich bags and styrofoam cups, are dumped into the world's oceans. This plastic waste is lethal, killing up to one million seabirds and 100,000 marine mammals a year.

Avoid over-packaged foods. Whenever you can, **buy fresh**, unpacked food instead. It will probably be **better for your health** as well as the environment. Don't take a plastic bag from the shopkeeper. **Take your own bag** to the shop if you need one.

 Put your rubbish in the recycling bin. **Look out for a 'recyclable' symbol**. Most steel and aluminium drink cans can be recycled (see page 145).

Many councils have special collections for recyclable rubbish.

1.00 p.m.

PHONE A FRIEND

In 2006, worldwide sales of new mobile phones topped **1,000 million**. It is estimated that there are five billion handsets in existence. One between every 1.3 people.

EVERY DAY COUNTS...

Like computers, mobile phones are slaves to changes in technology and fashion. We replace our handsets, on average, every 18 months.

Mobile phones contain a variety of highly toxic substances that have been linked to cancers and other disorders in humans. All of these substances can be released into the environment through landfills and incinerators. An old battery contains enough cadmium to contaminate 600,000 litres of water. Although much less toxic, tantalum (refined from the mineral coltan) causes damage to the environment at source. Tantalum is used in the electric circuitboards of phones.

Four-fifths of the world's supply of coltan is located in the war-torn Democratic Republic of Congo. To the east of the country, forests are being illegally cleared to dig coltan mines. This threatens a number of rare plants and animals with extinction.

The plastic covers of mobile phones last for hundreds of years in landfill sites. In Europe, 100 million mobile phones are discarded every year. If this continues, imagine how many phones will still be there in 100 years' time.

Many phone shops have a recycling bin for old handsets. You could also sell your old phone to a **recycling company** or send it through a charity such as Oxfam (see page 170). Many **useful parts can be reused**. Precious and semi-precious metals can be extracted, saving up to 90 per cent of the energy required to mine and refine raw metal ores.

Do you really need an upgrade? If your mobile phone still works, **give it another six months**, or even a year, before you trade it in for the latest model.

Don't leave your phone charger switched on. It wastes energy and is a potential fire risk because, even when not connected to a phone, a charger continues to draw electricity. Why not skip the mains completely and ask for a wind-up or **solar-powered charger** as a birthday or Christmas present?

Solar-powered chargers use energy from the Sun.

3.15 p.m.

GOING HOME

There are **16,000** kilometres of walking and cycle routes on traffic-free paths, quiet lanes and traffic-calmed roads in the UK. You probably live within 3 kilometres of a cycle route.

EVERY DAY COUNTS...

Short journeys by car are very damaging to the environment. Engines use more fuel in the first few kilometres of driving than later in the journey.

Cars continue to damage the planet when they are scrapped. Two million cars reach the end of their working lives in the UK every year. But thousands of tonnes of metals, glass and plastics are wasted instead of being recycled or reused.

There are many ways of reusing tyres. Some are used to replace the tread on the surface of other tyres. Some are shredded to surface sports grounds. Some are burned in kilns instead of coal to make cement. This creates fewer greenhouse gas emissions and means less waste is buried. However, there are fears that the fumes from the kilns are a health hazard. Illegal dumping still remains a problem. Thousands of tyres are removed from rivers each year.

EVERY DAY COUNTS...

It is often unnecessary and expensive to own a car in the city. **Public transport** in cities will get you about town faster and at a fraction of the cost to the environment. Even if your family owns a car, use buses, trams and trains whenever possible. The best way to get to and from school is by bicycle.

Your parents can **prolong the life** of their cars with regular maintenance and services. The tyres should always be at the right pressure and replaced before they wear out. Tyres that are reasonably healthy can be **used for retreading**. Making a retread tyre uses 20 litres less oil than making a new tyre.

FAIRTRADE

It is becoming more and more difficult for small traders to compete with multi-national companies. Fairtrade helps poor producers work their way out of poverty.

Fairtrade is a system of international trade that ensures people are paid a fair price for their produce, regardless of market forces, and that they have safe and good working conditions. The aim of Fairtrade is to reduce poverty and create opportunities for development among people who have been economically disadvantaged by the traditional trading systems. In these systems, fierce market competition and worldwide changes in demand affect the prices of goods and therefore the livelihoods of people across the globe. This is felt especially by farmers in the developing world.

FAIRTRADE LABELLING

Producers who meet the criteria set by the Fairtrade Labelling Organizations International (FLO) can be registered with the FLO. Brands that use products from registered Fairtrade producers can use the Fairtrade mark on their goods. When you see this mark on anything from fruit and vegetables to bars of chocolate and sports balls, you can be sure that the ingredients have been bought from internationally recognized Fairtrade sources.

THE ENVIRONMENT

Fairtrade items do not have to be organic, but many are. One of the Fairtrade criteria is that the environment is considered during production. Rainforest clearance is not practised and many pesticides are banned. Farmers are often paid more for produce that is certified as organic, so they have an incentive.

If there were no Fairtrade sales, many small coffee farmers would have to cut down their trees and give up. The current price of coffee in the conventional market does not cover their costs.

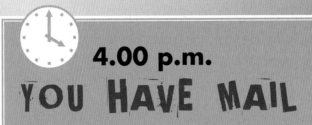

4.00 p.m.

YOU HAVE MAIL

240 kilograms of fossil fuels are burned to make just one desktop computer. The manufacturing process itself consumes 22 kilograms of chemicals and 1.5 tonnes of water.

EVERY DAY COUNTS

As technology advances and our appetite for high performance computers grows stronger, we end up scrapping millions of usable PCs every year.

Computers contain toxic elements such as lead, mercury and cadmium (the seventh most dangerous substance on Earth). If computers are dumped in landfill sites, these elements can leach into the soil and can make their way into groundwater. The use of these hazardous substances in computers is now heavily restricted in many countries.

EVERY DAY COUNTS...

Building computers is a particularly energy-intensive business. Weight for weight, it is around ten times less efficient than building a car or a refrigerator. A single memory chip uses 700 times its own weight in fuel during its construction. With so much energy and effort going into production, we can't afford to treat computers as a disposable commodity.

We replace our computers every few years whether or not they're still in working order. In the UK alone, some two million PCs will be discarded over the next 12 months as Waste Electrical and Electronic Equipment (WEEE). The problem is that computers, like many items of WEEE, contain non-biodegradable plastics and poisonous metallic elements.

About 13,400 million litres of oil are pumped out of the ground every day. When oil is burned as fuel to make items such as computers, an enormous amount of greenhouse gas goes into the atmosphere. And harmful chemicals made from oil are used to make some computer components.

Upgrade your computer or get a faulty unit **repaired**. If you buy new, choose the most advanced computer you can afford – it'll date less quickly. The most **energy-efficient machines** carry an Energy Star logo or the TCO label (from a Swedish organization that issues environmental and quality labels for computers, screens and keyboards).

You can **donate your old computer** to your school or give it to a friend. Alternatively, send your computer to an accredited recycling or refurbishing company.

Don't leave your computer running for 24 hours a day, and **switch off your monitor** when you have finished with it. It's been estimated that you could laser print 800 pages with the energy you waste by leaving on a computer monitor overnight.

4.30 p.m.

HOMEWORK

It is estimated that each year, every person in the UK throws away **two trees'** worth of paper and card.

EVERY DAY COUNTS

Thinking about what you do with waste will save you and your family money. It is key to reducing the impact you have on the environment.

In theory, paper comes from an infinitely renewable source, because trees can be replaced. However, timber forests are not always managed with the environment in mind. Trees that are not native to an area are often planted because they grow quickly and can therefore be sold quickly. Native wildlife then loses its natural habitat.

Although it is biodegradable, waste paper releases methane (a potent greenhouse gas) as it decomposes in landfills. New paper is often chlorine-bleached. Chlorine is a naturally occurring substance but when it is used in manufacturing processes, some poisonous by-products are created. These can contribute to major environmental problems including depletion of the ozone layer, global warming and acid rain.

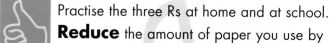

Practise the three Rs at home and at school. **Reduce** the amount of paper you use by correcting documents on your computer and avoid unnecessary printing. **Reuse** both sides of the paper and print draft documents on scrap. **Recycle** all of your waste paper.

Use only **Forest Stewardship Council** (FSC) certified virgin paper and card. The FSC promotes responsible stewardship of the world's forests. It certifies wood and paper only if it has been produced by practices that 'maintain the ecological functions and the **integrity of the forest**'.

Buy recycled paper. Each tonne of recycled paper can save 17 trees, enough electricity to heat your house for six months, nearly 32,000 litres of water and 2.3 cubic metres of landfill space.

6.00 p.m.

TEA TIME

Ten per cent of the greenhouse gases (including 25 per cent of the methane), emitted into our atmosphere is produced by livestock such as cattle and sheep.

EVERY DAY COUNTS...

Meat consumption per person has doubled in the last 50 years, and our increasingly carnivorous appetites are putting a considerable strain on the environment.

EVERY DAY COUNTS...

The farming of livestock results in atmospheric and water pollution. Greenhouse gas emissions and slurry run-off into rivers and streams are culprits, but the real problem is resources. Animals eat more food than they produce as edible meat. It takes 200 times the amount of water to produce 1 kilogram of beef as it does to grow 1 kilogram of soya – another source of protein.

Beef production is particularly damaging to the environment.

Waste from livestock, together with the fertilizers used to grow their feed, pollutes land, air and water with nitrates and ammonia, which damage ecosystems and destroy wildlife habitats.

You don't necessarily have to adopt a vegetarian or vegan (free of all animal products) diet to help save the planet. Just follow the advice of The Compassion in World Farming Trust and **eat less meat**. Try to buy organic meat from local farms.

Half the global harvest of
wheat, corn and soya is fed to
livestock. Crop farming is energy intensive
and we get back much less energy than we put
in – 10 tonnes of cattle feed leads to only
1 tonne of beef, for example.

How you cook is just as
important as what you cook.
Since 1970, the amount of energy we use in
the kitchen has fallen as more of us choose
convenient (and heavily packaged), take-away
foods. However, ovens and hobs still account
for 3.5 per cent of domestic energy use.

Water has a particularly high specific heat capacity, which means it requires a great deal of energy to warm it up. So you'll save energy by using less water and **cooking with steam**. Steam will do some of the work in an ordinary saucepan if you keep the water simmering and the **pan covered**.

Make sure your pan is the same size as, or slightly larger than, the ring on your hob. Note that a fan oven might use 20 per cent less energy than a conventional model, but a microwave will save almost 70 per cent. Grills can be very inefficient so **always toast bread in a toaster**.

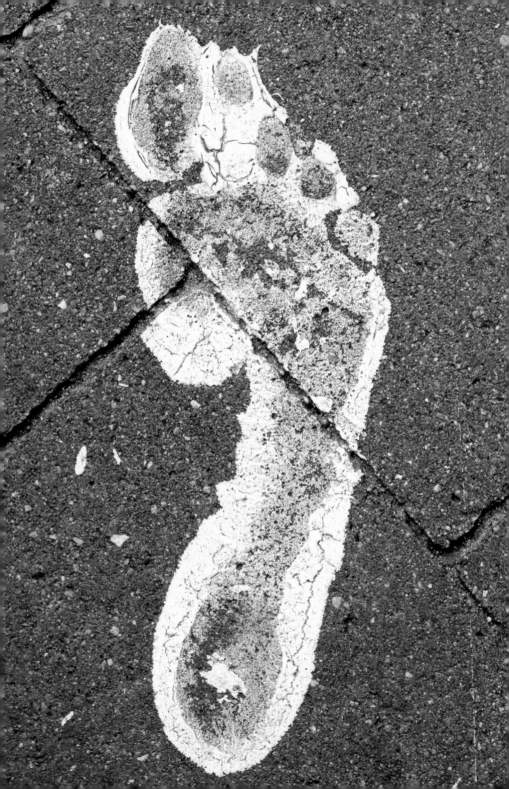

CARBON FOOTPRINT

Everyone leaves a carbon footprint. It is a measure of the impact an individual has on the environment through the emission of greenhouse gases.

Your carbon footprint is made up of two parts: the primary footprint and the secondary footprint. The primary footprint shows the emissions of carbon dioxide and other greenhouse gases for which you are directly responsible, such as those produced by travelling and using electricity. The secondary footprint is a measure of the emissions for which you are indirectly responsible, such as those produced by the manufacturing of goods that you buy. All these carbon dioxide emissions contribute to global warming.

MAKING A FOOTPRINT

The size of your carbon footprint depends on many factors. How you spend your free time is one of the most important. Do you watch TV and play video games, or do you read or play outdoors? Do you fly when you go on holiday? If you do, your footprint will be much larger than if you were to go by train. Rail travel is three times more fuel-efficient than air travel. Where your food comes from and how it was processed will affect your secondary footprint.

RESPONSIBILITIES

You may think you are not responsible for any emissions because your parents do all the shopping and choose the appliances in your home. And you may think that your school is responsible for everything

> The word 'footprint' is used because it makes us remember that through our actions we are leaving something behind, like a footprint in the sand, but for ever.

you do there. But you can try to persuade those in charge to change their habits. And you can watch less TV, turn off the light when you leave a room and unplug your mobile phone when it has finished charging. Each small action will help to make your footprint smaller.

6.30 p.m.

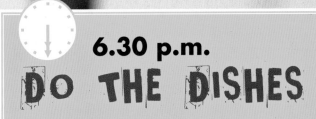

DO THE DISHES

Five litres of water gush from a running tap every minute – something to think about when you are rinsing the dishes. A dripping tap can waste up to 4 litres every day.

EVERY DAY COUNTS...

It may be a relief for you to know that dishwashers might actually be better for the environment than washing up everything by hand in the sink.

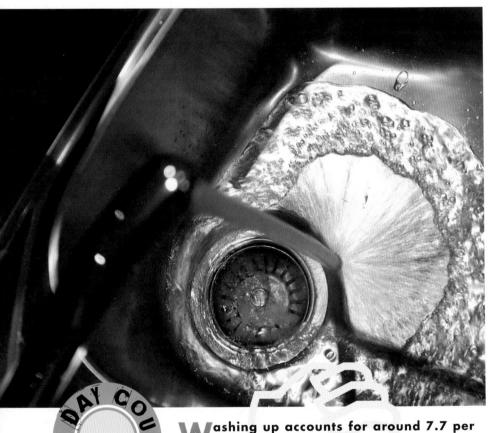

EVERY DAY COUNTS...

Washing up accounts for around 7.7 per cent of the water we use in our homes. Twenty-five per cent of families now own a dishwasher and will run it through, on average, 250 cycles a year.

The most efficient dishwashers require between one and two units of electricity (depending on the programme) for a full cycle. They will use only 15 litres of water. Washing a full load by hand can use anything from 30 to 200 litres.

Use your dishwasher only when you've collected enough for a **full load**. (Note that half-load programmes actually use more than 50 per cent of the water and energy of a full load.) You can save more energy by opening your machine early and allowing the contents to **air dry**.

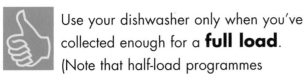

Don't pre-rinse crockery under a running tap. Instead, **scrape food scraps** into the bin shortly after a meal, so they haven't got a chance to dry hard on your plates, before loading the dishwasher or filling the sink.

Ordinary washing-up liquids and powders contain a mixture of chemicals. These pollute the environment. Tablets often come in too much packaging.

It's common practice to rinse soap suds off dishes under a running tap. That's why washing up by hand can use so much water.

Many of the ingredients of washing-up liquid are not biodegradable. They will exist forever, poisoning the environment.

EVERY DAY COUNTS...

Best practice for washing up by hand: fill two sinks (or bowls) – one with hot water and **eco-friendly washing-up liquid** for washing, and a second with cold water for rinsing. Use this **water on the garden** afterwards.

Using two sinks for washing up – one with soapy water, one with clean water for rinsing. You can rinse under a running tap to start with, while you fill the sink.

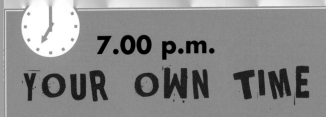

7.00 p.m.

YOUR OWN TIME

£740 million worth of energy is used every year by TVs, stereos and other electrical appliances left on standby. This releases four million tonnes of carbon dioxide.

EVERY DAY COUNTS...

If you switch off your electrical equipment at the mains every time you have finished using it, you could save millions of tonnes of fuel.

Not many people use videotapes any more. As we download more TV, film and music directly on to our computers or portable hard drives, it won't be much longer before CDs and DVDs become as outdated as vinyl records. Already, 45 tonnes of CDs are discarded every month.

More and more people are choosing to receive digital and satellite TV for a greater choice of programmes. Many of us now have some kind of 'set-top box' linked to our television, decoding the digital and satellite signals. These boxes are always switched on, or left on standby. They draw electricity all the time and therefore waste energy.

Be creative and transform your old CDs and DVDs into reflective decorations or excellent birdscarers in the garden.

Eight per cent of the energy supplied to households is wasted by idling electronic equipment. UK televisions consume £190 million worth of electricity waiting on standby every year.

Always switch off TVs, VCRs, DVD players, computers and stereos at the mains (at the plug) when not in use.

If your equipment breaks down, **see if it can be repaired** before deciding to buy a replacement. When buying new, as always, look for the **most energy-efficient models**. Flat-screen TVs are usually much bigger than conventional (CRT) TVs, and therefore use more energy, but are often more efficient. Liquid crystal display (LCD) TVs, for example, can use less energy than similar size CRT models.

To save energy, try spending one evening a week **not watching TV** or listening to your stereo. Instead, you could meet up with your family or friends, take up a new hobby, or **read a good book.**

9.00 p.m.

AND SO TO BED

One-third of household water is used to flush the toilet – that's 50 litres of water flushed down the drain by every one of us, every day.

...EVERY DAY COUNTS...

It's been an environmentally friendly day. You can keep protecting the planet while you get ready for bed.

Many bathroom products, including toothpaste and shampoo, contain palm oil. In order to establish palm oil plantations, the rainforests in Indonesia and Malaysia are being chopped down. This has caused the orangutan population to crash in the last 15 years. About 5000 orangutans die every year. Most companies don't know where their palm oil comes from but they could probably do more to find out.

About 60 per cent of tissue products, such as toilet paper and face tissues, contain no recycled fibres. Some of the 'virgin fibres' even come from ancient forests. Other tissue products actually contain more recycled fibres than they say. Manufacturers do not admit to the recycled fibres because they believe people would not buy the tissue, thinking it wasn't clean enough. But recycled fibres are made from office paper. They are scrubbed and washed many times before they go into the paper-making machine.

EVERY DAY COUNTS...

Don't leave the tap running when you clean your teeth. **Use a glass** or mug of water instead. If you haven't got a toilet with a water economy flush, **put a brick in your toilet cistern** so that the toilet uses less water per flush.

Use recycled tissue and check that it has not been bleached with chlorine. If you buy non-recycled, choose paper that is **FSC certified**.

Join the campaign to save the orangutan. Write to supermarkets and ask for their assurance and evidence that palm oil used in the products they sell **comes from a sustainable source**. Customer pressure can lead to action. You can find the addresses on the Safe Palm Oil website (see page 170).

WATER AND AIR POLLUTION

Water covers 75 per cent of the Earth's surface so it may seem silly to worry about saving it. But just 1 per cent of the Earth's water has to meet all our needs.

We are forced to rely on rainwater for all our water needs. The high salt content of seawater makes it undrinkable and too corrosive for most industrial or agricultural projects. The salt can be taken out, but the process is energy intensive and a threat to seawater habitats.

Three million people are killed by air pollution every year. More than two million die from diseases associated with unsafe water.

WATER DEMAND

The world's population is growing. Our demand for pure, clean water is increasing, and yet climate changes and pollution threaten to reduce our supplies. Purifying water for domestic consumption becomes increasingly difficult as we flush and drain away toxic chemicals from our homes. We pollute the atmosphere – and therefore rainwater – with emissions from industry and transport. Industrial and agricultural water pollution harms wildlife and habitats. Artificial chemical fertilizers and pesticides poison marine life, including fish and animals that we eat.

AIR POLLUTION

Burning fossil fuels releases sulphur dioxide – a gas that can acidify rainwater, creating 'acid rain'. This flows into lakes and rivers, affecting plants and animals. It damages trees, slowing their growth and burning their leaves brown, often leading to their death. Other fossil fuel fumes choke urban areas, reacting with sunlight to produce ground-level ozone. This 'bad ozone' affects people's lungs as well as damaging plant life and ecosystems. 'Good ozone' in the upper atmosphere absorbs harmful ultraviolet radiation from the Sun. But this layer of ozone has been damaged by air pollution.

9.30 p.m.
LiGHTS OUT

If **three** traditional light bulbs in every UK household were swapped for energy-efficient bulbs, it would save enough energy to light all the street lamps in the country.

EVERY DAY COUNTS...

We flood our cities with light, leave bulbs burning in empty rooms and use old technologies although energy-efficient alternatives are available.

Traditional tungsten filament bulbs are incredibly inefficient. They convert much more energy into heat than into light, which is why they get so hot. Switching to energy-efficient bulbs, such as LEDs (Light Emitting Diodes) or CFLs (Compact Fluorescent Lamps) can save up to 30 per cent of the electricity needed to light your home.

Fridges and freezers are two of the most energy-hungry appliances, and we have to keep them running all day and night. Some of them use coolants called hydrofluorocarbons (HFCs) which are greenhouse gases thousands of times more powerful than carbon dioxide. They have to be removed by specialists before the units can be recycled.

Light pollution is another problem. Wasted energy shining from all our towns and cities disorientates wildlife, disrupting sleep patterns and breeding cycles.

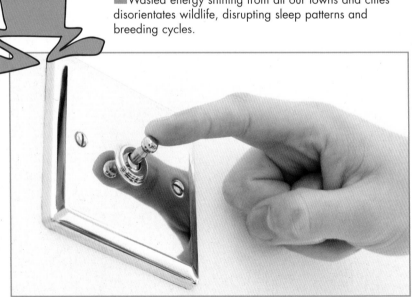

Don't leave on any lights overnight unless you absolutely have to. Persuade your parents to **replace** burned-out bulbs with **CFLs**, which last about ten times longer than traditional bulbs. As well as saving energy, they will save your family money on the electricity bill.

Save electricity by keeping warm at night under a thick duvet or blanket instead of turning up the heating. Use a **hot-water bottle** instead of an electric blanket. A wind-up alarm clock saves power wasted by a digital display.

Suggest that your family switches to green electricity. Most major suppliers offer green tariffs – pledging to generate a percentage of your electricity from **renewable sources** (see page 123).

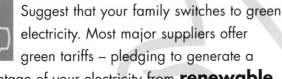

Offer to **defrost the fridge and freezer** regularly to keep them operating efficiently. Let cooked food cool before you put it in the fridge. If your parents are buying a new appliance, remind them to choose one that is **'A' rated or better, for energy efficiency**, and is guaranteed HFC-free.

WEEKENDS

Saving the planet doesn't have to be difficult or inconvenient. Once you get into the habit it will become second nature.

At weekends, you probably have time to help out around the house and in the garden! This gives you and your family and friends lots of opportunities to save the planet. You may not be able to try out every suggestion.

Exercise is important to keep you fit and healthy, but remember to consider your effect on the environment while you enjoy yourself.

KEEP IT GOING

This section takes you through Saturday and Sunday when you catch up on household chores, look after your pets and go out with your friends. You will find out what food miles are (see page 108), what alternative energy sources exist (see page 123) and how you can recycle your waste (see page 145). Don't forget to continue with the actions you now take to save the planet during a school day.

Saturday

LOAD THE WASHING MACHINE

£800 million

of electricity is needed
to pass 500 billion litres of
water through washing
machines, tumble dryers and
dishwashers
across the UK,
every year.

EVERY DAY COUNTS...

White goods (washing machines, fridges, cookers and dishwashers) harm the environment throughout their working lives and long after they've been taken to the scrap heap.

A **washing machine is part of the fixtures and fittings in most households.** Each machine will perform nearly 300 cycles a year – with each cycle using anything from 50 to 120 litres of water. This is around 14 per cent of the water used in homes.

M **any of the detergents we use to get our clothes whiter eventually reach natural waterways and the sea.** Some detergents take decades to break down completely and the phosphates present in many common powders choke the marine environment by stimulating algal growth.

E **uropeans dispose of 6.5 million tonnes of Waste Electronic and Electrical Equipment (WEEE), every year.** In the UK alone, over a million tonnes end up as landfill. Since 2003, the European Union's WEEE Directive has aimed to cut down on toxic 'e-waste' by encouraging the reuse and recycling of such products.

When you help with the washing, wait till you **have a full load** before you put a wash on. As most modern detergents work at 40°C, there's no need to wash clothes at higher temperatures. A 40°C cycle will **use half the energy** of one at 65°C.

Use environmentally friendly detergents and avoid the temptation to tumble dry your clothes. If possible, **hang them outside** and let the wind and sun do the work! And if your clothes are only lightly soiled, hang them outside on a clothesline to freshen them up. This **saves the need** for an extra wash.

White goods account for almost half our WEEE. When your washing machine breaks down, suggest to your parents that they **get it repaired**. If they buy a replacement, tell them to look for models carrying the European Eco-Label, the Energy Saving Recommended Logo or those rated A or A+ for **energy efficiency**.

Saturday

SHOP FOR FOOD

The average item of food you see in a supermarket has travelled more than **1,600 kilometres**. That's further than driving from one end of the UK to the other.

EVERY DAY COUNTS...

Supermarkets are the most convenient places to do the weekly shop. Some things appear cheap, but what is the real cost of food?

EVERY DAY COUNTS

The environmental costs of importing and transporting food are huge. The problem is getting worse as many countries cannot produce enough food for their increasing populations and are forced to import more food every year. Even fresh produce is taken to packaging and processing plants across the country before it reaches the supermarket.

Choose loose fruits and vegetables instead of those in plastic bags and trays. Avoid over-packaged snacks and ready-made meals. **Buy less canned** and bottled food and avoid packaging that consists of mixed materials (eg paper and plastic and foil) because they are too expensive to recycle.

Food that can't be grown in the UK, such as bananas, travels thousands of miles to get to your shopping basket.

> Have a look in your fridge next time it's full of food and see where all the items come from. You may be surprised how many miles your next meal has clocked up!

Some foodstuffs will never be grown locally, and some shouldn't be. For example, it is estimated that it's more environmentally friendly to import tomatoes into the UK from Spain than to grow them here in heated greenhouses. But it is not necessary to import apples during the apple season – which is what some supermarkets do. Although supermarkets stock a wide range of organic food, around 56 per cent of this produce will be imported.

Supermarket lorries travel 1,080 million kilometres every year transporting goods, much of which is food. The total number of food miles (see page 108) increases with each customer. The average adult drives 220 kilometres a year to shop for food.

Take a walk to your local store or farmers' market to buy locally produced (and, therefore, in season) organic food. There are many companies that **deliver reusable boxes** of organic food straight to your door – much more fun than following your parents around the supermarket!

Look for places where you can **pick your own** organic fruit and vegetables. This **saves food miles** and you know the food is fresh. If you have a garden, encourage your family to grow its own vegetables.

FOOD MILES

The distance food travels to your plate is measured in food miles. Food transport adds to the carbon dioxide emissions that are contributing to global warming.

Food miles include the journey food takes from the farmer to the processor, from the processor to the packager, from the packager to the shop and from the shop to the consumer. This journey may involve transport from one country to another, but lots of food travels long distances within one country. Fresh produce is imported from all over the world. Heavily processed foods, like ready-made meals, might contain ingredients sourced from many different countries.

Food travels further today partly because people prefer to do all their

country. It's possible that a potato can travel many miles to be packaged and then be transported back to near where it was grown! Of course, all this travelling costs money, and this is added to the price you pay for the potato.

CONSUMER RESPONSIBILITY

It is not just supermarkets that are responsible for food miles. The journey from the supermarket to your home counts too. So next time one of your family wants something to eat, encourage them to walk to the local shop to get it rather than drive to the supermarket.

95 per cent of the fruit and 50 per cent of the vegetables eaten in the UK are imported.

FOOD MILES ARE HARMFUL

There are many reasons why it is important to reduce the number of miles that food travels. The harm done to the environment by burning fuel is a major one, and there are issues of human health and animal welfare too. The further food travels, the less fresh it is. It loses vitamins and its nutritional value decreases. The well-being of live animals that are transported, sometimes for days from one country to another, must also be considered.

shopping at a supermarket rather than at lots of different shops. And it is best for the supermarkets if they get their food packaged at one central depot, which then delivers it to branches around the

Saturday

YOUR BEST FRIEND

500 million tropical fish, almost 10 million reptiles, 2.5 million birds and 30,000 primates are caught and exported every year as 'exotic pets'.

EVERY DAY COUNTS...

Hundreds of animals are shipped around the world every day to be sold. This is stressful, especially for animals that have been captured illegally from the wild.

So-called 'exotic pets' are difficult to keep happy and healthy because it's often impossible to replicate their natural habitats in the home. Reptiles, for example, require highly specific temperature, light and humidity levels as well as a specialized diet – 15 per cent of pet lizards have been found to suffer from malnutrition.

All pets need regular exercise and an adequate, nutritious diet. Sadly, some owners fail to meet these demands – around a third of UK pets are now overweight. Others find it too difficult to commit the necessary time and effort to pet-care. In 2006, UK local authorities had to deal with more than 100,000 stray dogs.

Millions of pet dogs produce thousands of tonnes of excrement every day. This creates more than just a litter problem. Dog faeces contain the roundworm, *Toxocara* (as many as one million eggs in every stool). The parasite can exist for up to two years in the soil and, if ingested, can lead to blindness in humans.

This is a warning to dog owners that dog pooping is prohibited in this area!

Before inviting an animal to join your family, **make sure** you have the space and can afford the time to look after it. **Consider adopting** a rescued animal. Be sure to vaccinate, worm and neuter your pets.

Pick up after your dog. Freshly deposited faeces are not immediately infectious and can be safely pooper-scooped into the nearest designated dog bin. If you can't find a dog bin nearby, (double) wrap the mess in a carrier bag and **dispose of it at home**.

Cats will prey on small birds and mammals. You can help to **limit the damage** they do to your local ecosystem by keeping them in (or out of) your garden with cat-proof fencing. Introduce **prickly plants** around the base of bird tables or sprinkle orange peel in flower beds.

Saturday

READY TO GO OUT

For every **10 grams** of gold extracted (enough for a single ring), 18 tonnes of waste ore are created. Metal mining is one of the most polluting activities on the planet.

EVERY DAY COUNTS...

It's important that anyone who wears accessories knows where the materials have come from and considers the real cost of fashionable metals and jewels.

Some people choose not to wear any leather shoes and belts, or carry a leather bag or wallet because of the issue of animal welfare. The tanning process of leather can also release toxic chemicals. But many leather alternatives have their own environmental problems.

Extracting metals from rocks threatens natural habitats and biodiversity. Land has to be cleared for mines and some ores are refined using harmful chemicals. Gold, for example, is extracted through a process whereby cyanide is washed through the ore to bond with and separate out the gold. The cyanide contaminates the environment. A host of other pollutants, already present in the ore (including mercury, arsenic and lead), also drain into groundwater.

Conflict diamonds are those that are illegally traded to fund conflict in war-torn areas. The Kimberley Process Certification Scheme was launched in 2003 to block international trade in conflict gems. Now 99 per cent of the world's diamonds are from conflict-free sources. But 1 per cent is still being illegally smuggled.

There are now several companies that make **organic leather** items. The hides used are from animals that are fed organic food and humanely raised. The tanning process uses plant tannins or smoke so there is **zero toxicity**.

If you are lucky enough to get jewellery as a present consider conflict as well as colour, cut and carat. Jewellery should come with a **written guarantee** that the gems are conflict-free.

Choose jewellery made from **recycled metals** (or metals sourced in the most ecologically responsible way). Look for **Fairtrade jewellery** or buy items made from alternative, environmentally sound materials.

Buy fewer new clothes and accessories. Have a look in **charity shops**. If you search carefully you will find some good-quality items and some amazing bargains. And don't forget to take your own cast-offs to a charity shop or put them in a **clothing bank**. You can recycle shoes too.

SAVE YOUR PLANET...

Sunday

HOW CLEAN IS YOUR HOUSE?

72,000 synthetic chemicals have been introduced into multi-surface cleaners, bleaches, toiletries and a host of other products since the 1950s.

You are careful about what you put on your skin and wash with, but do you think about the cleaning products you come into contact with every day?

More and more people are sterilizing their homes with anti-bacterial sprays and chlorine bleaches. These are supposed to protect us, but can lead to the evolution of antibiotic-resistant bacteria. The sprays kill weaker bacteria more easily, leading to natural selection of stronger, more dangerous bacteria.

Chlorine bleaches are disinfectants commonly found in cleaning powders and liquids. They are highly caustic, meaning they can burn skin and eyes, and when they travel from your drain into the environment they can produce carcinogenic (cancer-causing) chemicals called dioxins.

Persistent synthetic chemicals are used in many cleaning products. They refuse to break down, or biodegrade slowly. When they find their way into the sea, they build up in the bodies of marine organisms and enter the food chain. The chemical Triclosan, for example, has been found in fish and human breast milk.

Chemicals called phthalates are used in surface-cleaners, cosmetics and flexible plastic products. Scientists suspect that they affect the hormone systems in animals, and have linked them to reproductive problems in wildlife.

You should wear rubber gloves when using cleaning products to protect your hands from chemicals.

Use cleaning products made with all **natural ingredients** from renewable sources, where possible. Environmentally **friendly** toilet and surface cleaners are available.

 Alternatively, see if you can **make your own** cleaning products. Diluted white wine vinegar, lemon juice and baking soda can be used separately or together to clean a variety of surfaces, windows and tiles. Olive oil, mixed with a dash of vinegar, makes an effective furniture polish.

Ask if you can use **household borax** for cleaning, which is very effective as an antibacterial, fungicidal and bleaching agent. It is ideal for tackling stubborn stains and has very **low toxicity**. It can be used safely in toilets, on carpets and even in the washing machine to boost the power of the powder.

ALTERNATIVE ENERGY SOURCES

In the UK, coal, oil and natural gas-fired power stations are responsible for the largest share of carbon dioxide emissions.

Not only does the burning of fossil fuels threaten to accelerate global warming, but the world's limited supplies of coal, oil and natural gas are in danger of running out altogether. Nuclear power is one alternative. Several renewable energy sources have also been developed. They have low or even no carbon emissions, and will either never run out or can be regenerated in a short period of time.

NUCLEAR POWER

Nuclear power is the production of electricity using an assortment of radioactive metals, such as uranium and plutonium, as 'nuclear fuel'. Under certain conditions, these metals produce enough heat energy to turn water into steam, which is then used to drive turbines and generate electricity. Carbon dioxide is not produced as a by-product of this process. Moreover, nuclear fuel can be seen as a sustainable energy source in the medium to long term because radioactive fuels are relatively plentiful and reprocessing can transform spent material back into usable fuel. Of course, nuclear power is not without its problems. A certain amount of highly radioactive, toxic, irrecoverable waste is produced by the process, raising the issue of how to dispose of it safely. Accidents in power stations do not happen often, but they can result in massive environmental contamination. There is also concern that the technology behind nuclear power can be adapted to create nuclear weapons, and that the power stations are targets for terrorist attacks.

GREEN ENERGY

There are five main types of renewable, or 'green' energy: solar, hydro (water), wind, geothermal and biomass. Energy from the Sun can be captured using solar panels. Some types of solar panel convert the energy into electricity. Others use it to heat buildings and water directly.

The Earth's natural heat can also be used to generate electricity or heat buildings directly. In Iceland, geothermal energy supplies water at 86°C to 95 per cent of buildings in the capital Reykjavik.

Hydroelectric power stations use water, moving under gravity, to drive huge engines called turbines to generate electricity.

> Most wind turbines start generating electricity at wind speeds of 3–4 metres per second.

Wind power is one of the cleanest and safest methods of generating electricity on a large scale. In the UK, wind farms consisting of hundreds of large turbines built on land and offshore have the potential to provide 10 per cent of our power needs over the next 20 years.

Energy scientists use the term biomass to describe any plant or animal material that can be burned to release energy. Wood, crop waste such as straw, and animal dung are examples of biomass that can be burned to produce energy. This releases carbon dioxide, but unlike burning fossil fuels it doesn't add any extra carbon into the environment. The carbon dioxide is absorbed by new trees and crops planted to renew the biomass fuel, which is why biomass is described as 'carbon neutral'. It does not contribute to global warming.

Wind farms consist of large turbines driven by the wind.

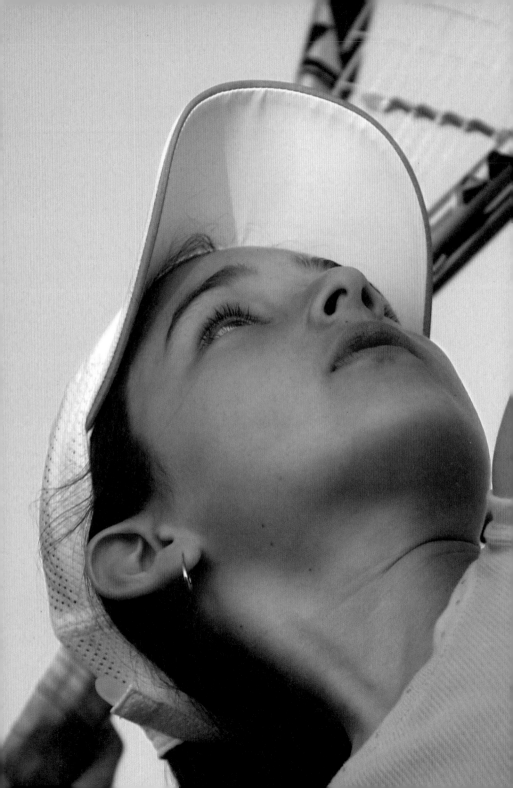

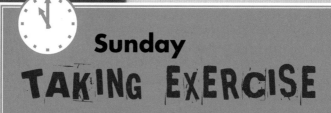

Sunday

TAKING EXERCISE

About **6 million** litres of water are used in showers and swimming pools in the average leisure centre every year. Much of this is heated.

EVERY DAY COUNTS...

Regular exercise keeps us healthier for longer – reducing the demands we place on our health service. But make sure you exercise in a way that benefits the environment as well as yourself.

Leisure centre members use an enormous amount of energy playing sport and working out in gyms. But the leisure centres themselves use much more energy for lighting and heating and for powering equipment.

Some sports clubs install water-coolers to dispense ice-cold water into wasteful, plastic cups. Many of us bring our own water in plastic bottles. The process of bottling and transporting water to areas where a safe supply of mains water already exists wastes natural resources and damages the environment. There is little to justify the food miles clocked up by the 89 billion litres of bottled water sold each year (22 billion litres are exported outside their country of origin), and the 1.5 million tonnes of PVC and other plastics used to make the bottles.

Don't go to the leisure centre or sports club in a car. If possible, **walk there or cycle**. This will warm up your muscles before you do any major exercising and will also save on carbon dioxide emissions.

 Wash and reuse empty drinks bottles. Fill them with tap water and take them with you instead of buying bottled water. And if you want cold water, fill a bottle and store it in the fridge in advance **instead of running the tap** until the water gets cold. This **saves water**.

Get some exercise by taking part in conservation activities. Your friends or family could help with a local project, such as canal clearing, creating a nature area or tree planting.

 Take **exercise outdoors** rather than indoors as often as possible. An outdoor tennis court, for example, does **not need lighting** during the day.

Sunday

HOW GREEN IS YOUR GARDEN?

1,000 litres of water can be used by a garden sprinkler in just one hour. That's enough water for you to have about 12 baths or 28 showers.

EVERY DAY COUNTS...

Helping your family to create a 'green' garden will encourage wildlife and give you lots of opportunities to conserve resources and recycle waste.

Plants need watering in dry weather or they will die. Dry weather is becoming more common, possibly because of climate change. Many people use a sprinkler to water the garden. It is better to water the garden generously only when absolutely necessary, rather than little and often. If there is a severe water shortage, water companies often impose a hosepipe ban, which includes sprinklers.

Persuade your family to **get a water butt** in which to collect rainwater for use in the garden. You can also get a system to filter and **reuse 'grey' water** from the kitchen and bathroom. Water plants and shrubs in the cool of the morning or early evening, to minimize losses from evaporation.

If there is a hosepipe ban and you are asked to water the garden use a watering can instead.

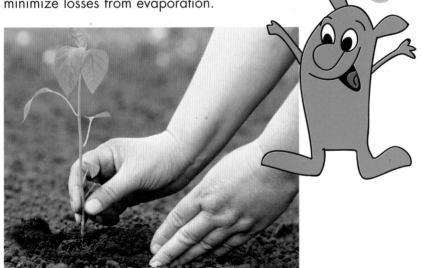

A patch of wild flowers in the garden will encourage insects and other wildlife to visit.

Soil often needs a bit of help to nourish plants but commercial fertilizers can do more harm than good. Many of them contain ammonia, which is made using natural gas as a source of both energy and hydrogen. (Natural gas is a fossil fuel and it releases carbon dioxide when it's burned.) Nitrates in fertilizers wash into rivers and disrupt aquatic ecosystems.

Pests such as slugs, snails and caterpillars can be a problem in the garden, eating all your favourite plants. But as well as killing the pests, pesticides also kill helpful animals that you want to keep. Commercial ones damage the soil and some cause health problems in humans.

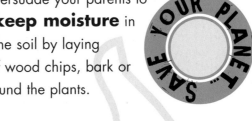

Persuade your parents to **keep moisture** in the soil by laying mulches of wood chips, bark or gravel around the plants.

Organic fertilizers are available to buy or you can **make compost** using organic scraps from the kitchen and garden.

There are also 'natural' pest control items for sale. But try making **your own spray** of liquid soap or garlic mixed with water. Suggest you have plants in the garden that repel certain pests or attract **pest-eating insects**. Slugs can be caught in beer traps or eradicated using nematode worms – a natural, biological pest control.

Sunday

HELPING WITH DIY

20 per cent of the 40 millions of litres of paint sold every year in the UK will never be used. We stockpile millions of litres of paint in garages and throw away millions more.

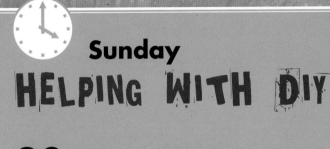

EVERY DAY COUNTS...

For some, DIY is good fun; for others it is a pain in the neck. For the environment, DIY uses up natural resources and is a source of chemical pollutants.

Solvent-based paints contain chemicals known as **Volatile Organic Compounds, or VOCs.** Volatile means they vaporize easily and enter the atmosphere. A number of VOCs are, in themselves, toxic or carcinogenic. Almost all cause ground-level ozone and, indirectly, contribute to the enhanced greenhouse effect.

The chemistry behind water-based paints can be even more energy intensive and ecologically hazardous. As much as 40 million litres of water is needed to dilute just one litre of water-soluble gloss paint before it is considered safe enough to wash through the sewers.

By redesigning and improving our homes we produce 420,000 tonnes of waste wood each year. Much of this is 'timber composite' wood, including medium-density fibreboard (MDF) and chipboard. These are made of wood fibres glued together. These products are difficult to recycle, their manufacture is energy intensive, and they contain a variety of harmful chemicals.

The first rule of DIY is to **repair and restore** what you already have and, wherever possible, to make use of recycled or reclaimed materials. If your family needs to buy new wood, choose **Forest Stewardship Council** (FSC)-certified timber – preferably from local forests. The FSC is an international organization that promotes socially and environmentally **responsible forest management**.

 Persuade your family to buy paint made from **natural, organic materials**. Paints and wood varnishes are available that contain natural **plant and animal pigments** and no petrochemicals. If you have any paint left over, give it to a community or charity project.

You can have fun going to a reclamation centre to buy items for your home. **Reclaimed items** have been rescued from old houses. They range from door knockers to paving stones, from furniture to fireplaces.

Sunday

TAKE THE RUBBISH OUT

In a year, each person produces **ten times** their own weight in household rubbish: 160 cans, 107 bottles and jars, two trees' worth of paper and 45 kilograms of plastic.

EVERY DAY COUNTS...

We can all help protect the world's natural resources. To get the most from our raw materials we must reduce, reuse and recycle household rubbish.

Most household rubbish is buried in the ground in landfill sites. Every year, we fill about 300 million square metres of land with rubbish. 28,450 football pitches would fit over the same area. Space is running out.

Metals (from waste foils, empty cans and aerosols) make up 8 per cent of our domestic rubbish. Metal mining and extraction are incredibly energy intensive industries. Recycling 1 tonne of aluminium saves around 14,000 kWh (kilowatt-hours) of electricity.

Rubbish dumped on our streets costs £500 million every year to clean up. Not only does it look horrible but it attracts rats and is a health hazard. Gum is especially difficult and expensive to remove, and it does not biodegrade. Methods used to remove it include high-pressure water and steam. These can damage the grouting between paving stones and even melt tarmac! They also use large amounts of energy. Using chemicals can be dangerous to health.

EVERY DAY COUNTS...

 The most important thing to do is **reduce** the amount of waste you produce. After that try to **reuse** as much as possible. Then think about recycling. If you don't have a recycling collection in your area, take as much of your rubbish as possible to your nearest recycling centre. Always **separate** paper, glass, plastic and metal items in your rubbish.

When you have to throw away rubbish or gum, don't just drop it on the ground. Put it in a **litter bin**. If you get caught dropping litter you may be fined.

Set up a **recycling committee** at your school to make sure that everyone in the school – including staff – knows about the recycling systems in place in your area. Try to persuade your school to have bins for recycling paper and to buy recycled paper in the first place.

RECYCLING YOUR RUBBISH

Over half the contents of your dustbin could be recycled or turned into compost. At present we recycle less than one-quarter of our domestic waste.

Recycling has many benefits for the environment. By recycling we reduce our rubbish, create less pollution and save energy. And we reduce the need to take raw materials from the earth. Most of these are non-renewable, meaning they cannot be replaced. Eventually the raw materials will run out. The process of extracting raw materials damages the environment and wildlife habitats. Then there are the problems associated with manufacturing and distributing new goods for you to buy to replace those you have thrown away.

WHAT CAN BE RECYCLED?

You may already know that glass, paper, aluminium and steel cans, textiles and organic waste can all be recycled. But did you know that plastic, electrical equipment and furniture can also be recycled? You can check with your council to find out what recycling schemes it runs. Or do some research on the Internet to discover what specialist recycling organizations exist. There are hundreds of websites with useful information. Most councils now run collection schemes to pick up material from outside your home.

RECYCLING EVERYDAY ITEMS

Glass

You will find bottle banks in many supermarket car parks and other public areas. They usually have bins for green, clear and brown glass. Remove as many tops as possible, but the labels will be removed in the recycling process.

Paper

The most common type of paper in your waste will be newspapers and magazines. These can go into the paper bank. Do not put cardboard or junk mail in here. You may find a bank specially for these. Milk and juice cartons cannot be recycled because they have a plastic lining.

Recycle your organic waste on a compost heap in the garden or in a compost bin.

Drink and food cans

Try to crush the cans before putting them in the bank. There may be a special bank for aluminium cans because these have a higher value. They have a very shiny silver base and do not stick to magnets.

KEEP A DIARY

You know what you can do to help save the planet. This diary will help you to plan a new routine and stick to it.

Use the following diary pages to record your impact on the environment. The left-hand pages are for environmentally unfriendly actions, and the right-hand pages are for environmentally friendly deeds. Every time you do something on the list, put a cross or a tick on the relevant line. At the end of each month, add up the number of ticks or crosses in each row. Give yourself 1 point for each tick on a pale row, 2 points for each tick on a medium row and 3 points for each tick on a dark row. See if you can collect fewer bad points and more good points each month.

Don't worry if you find it difficult to build up good points at first. Saving the planet takes perseverance and determination.

GET YOUR FAMILY INVOLVED

Download a copy of the diary pages (see websites page 166) and ask your family, friends or classmates to keep a diary too. You could compare notes at the end of each month to see who is doing their bit for the planet – and who is not.

MONTH 1

Put a cross every time you...

have a deep bath

have a lift in the car to school on your own

buy some crisps and snacks to eat

leave your mobile phone charger plugged in

throw away paper that could have been recycled

buy some bottled water

turn up the heating instead of wearing more layers

put your clothes in the tumble dryer

leave the water running while brushing your teeth

drop some litter on the ground

Ooooh you've been bad!

1 point

2 points

3 points

Put a tick every time you...

have a quick shower

remember to turn off
a computer monitor

read a book instead of
watching TV

remind your family to check
the pressure of their car tyres

buy something certified
by the Soil Association

take some bottles or
cans to be recycled

buy local, organic
or Fairtrade food

make some pesticide
for the garden (page 135)

find a new outfit in
a charity shop

persuade your family to buy
energy-efficient light bulbs

1 point

2 points

3 points

You've been very good!

MONTH 2

Put a cross every time you...

have a deep bath

drop some litter
on the ground

leave the water running
while washing up

leave your mobile phone
charger plugged in

throw away paper that
could have been recycled

leave the water running
while brushing your teeth

turn up the heating instead
of wearing more layers

put your clothes in the
tumble dryer

buy some
bottled water

leave the lights on when
you are not in the room

*Hmmm
... that's
pretty bad.*

1 point

2 points

3 points

Put a tick every time you...

have a quick shower

remember to turn off
a computer monitor

read a book instead of
watching TV

hang up washing
to dry outside

make your own lunch
to take to school

take some bottles or
cans to be recycled

buy local, organic
or Fairtrade food

find out where to recycle
something in your area

walk or cycle somewhere
instead of having a lift

get something repaired
instead of buying a new one

Keep up the good work.

1 point

2 points

3 points

MONTH 3

Put a cross every time you...

have a deep bath

drop some litter
on the ground

take a plastic carrier
bag from a shop

leave your mobile phone
charger plugged in

throw away paper that
could have been recycled

leave the water running
while brushing your teeth

turn up the heating instead
of wearing more layers

water the garden or wash
a car with a hose or sprinkler

buy some
bottled water

have a lift somewhere
instead of walking

*Ooooh!
Still too many
bad points!*

1 point

2 points

3 points

Put a tick every time you...

have a quick shower

remember to turn off
a computer monitor

do a sport or hobby instead
of watching TV

check that the boiler thermostat
is set no higher than 60°C

follow the washing up
instructions on page 79

take some bottles or
cans to be recycled

buy local, organic
or Fairtrade food

make your own household
cleaners (page 121)

swap something with a friend
instead of buying new ones

take public transport
instead of having a lift

You can do even better than this!

1 point

2 points

3 points

MONTH 4

Put a cross every time you...

have a deep bath

leave the tap running
while doing the dishes

buy pre-packaged food instead
of making your own lunch

leave your mobile phone
charger plugged in

throw away paper that
could have been recycled

leave the water running
while brushing your teeth

leave a pan lid off while
boiling water to cook

leave a stereo or games
console switched on at the wall

buy some
bottled water

drop some gum
on the ground

It could be worse I suppose.

1 point

2 points

3 points

Put a tick every time you...

have a quick shower

remember to turn off
a computer monitor

read a book instead
of watching TV

walk, cycle or use public
transport instead of going by car

repair something around
the house

take some bottles or
cans to be recycled

wash and reuse
a drinks bottle

look around the house for
draughts that can be blocked

put a brick in a toilet
cistern in your house

write to an organization or
corporation about a green issue

Looks
like a good
effort!

1 point

2 points

3 points

MONTH 5

Put a cross every time you...

have a deep bath

throw some litter
on the ground

take a plastic carrier
bag from a shop

leave your mobile phone
charger plugged in

throw away paper that
could have been recycled

leave the water running
while brushing your teeth

turn up the heating instead
of wearing more layers

spend a whole evening
watching TV

buy some
bottled water

buy fast food or canned
soft drinks

*See
if you can do
better next
month.*

1 point

2 points

3 points

Put a tick every time you...

have a quick shower

remember to turn off
a computer monitor

meet friends instead of
watching TV

arrange to share lifts
with a friend's family

buy a card or paper product
that is FSC-certified

take some bottles or
cans to be recycled

buy local, organic
or Fairtrade food

encourage birds to visit your home
or school garden (page 113)

take some old clothes
to a clothing bank

set up a scheme to reuse or recycle
paper at school (page 143)

You're getting the idea.

1 point

2 points

3 points

MONTH 6

Put a cross every time you...

have a deep bath

throw some litter
on the ground

buy some crisps and
snacks to eat

leave your mobile phone
charger plugged in

leave a computer monitor
switched on overnight

leave the water running
while brushing your teeth

turn up the heating instead
of wearing more layers

put your clothes in the
tumble dryer

buy some
bottled water

ask for a lift instead of
walking or cycling

You should have fewer bad points by now.

1 point

2 points

3 points

Put a tick every time you...

have a quick shower

remember to turn off
a computer monitor

read a book instead of
watching TV

check a food label to make
sure it is locally made

use both sides of the paper
when printing a document

take some bottles or
cans to be recycled

try to buy food with
less packaging

set up a school collection scheme
for old mobile phones (page 50)

make compost using kitchen
or garden waste

give someone a lesson
in driving smoothly (page 39)

You
will help to
save the
planet!

1 point

2 points

3 points

GLOSSARY

Many of the terms used to describe the problems facing the planet may be new to you. This glosssary will help you to understand them.

ACID RAIN
When oxides of nitrogen and sulphur (compounds of oxygen with nitrogen or sulphur) are released into the atmosphere, they dissolve in water to produce nitric and sulphuric acid. This falls as acid rain, which damages buildings and trees. It also changes the nature of soil, making it unsuitable for plants and agriculture.

ALGAL BLOOM
When nitrogen or phosphorous-based nutrients are washed into reservoirs and other bodies of water, they cause algae populations to swell in an algal bloom. **Organisms** on the reservoir bed feed on the increased mass of dead algae. The bloom and other organisms remove oxygen from the water. If oxygen levels drop below the limit necessary to support aquatic life the reservoir is suffocated.

ALTERNATIVE FUEL VEHICLES
These include vehicles that run on liquid petroleum gas (LPG), compressed natural gas (CNG) or electricity. LPG is taken from refined **petroleum** or natural gas but LPG cars emit less carbon dioxide than petrol and fewer particulates (soot etc.). Electric cars cause no pollution themselves, but the electricity is generated elsewhere and often through the burning of **fossil fuels**. Hybrid cars use a combination of electric and petrol/gas power.

ARSENIC
A toxic element, classified as carcinogenic (causes cancer) to humans by the International Agency for Research on Cancer (IARC). It can be fatal to humans and wildlife if inhaled, swallowed or absorbed through the skin.

BIOACCUMULATIVE
Toxic substances are described as bioaccumulative when they build up in the bodies of organisms. These substances may not kill immediately, or in small quantities, but as they bioaccumulate, they will poison an organism over a period of time.

BIODEGRADABLE
Items that are biodegradable can be broken down by living **organisms**. This means they rot safely and relatively quickly. They disappear naturally into the environment.

BIODIESEL
A **biodegradable**, non-toxic, **carbon-neutral** fuel made from waste cooking oil and oilseed crops, including rapeseed. It can be used, without modifications, in most new diesel vehicles.

BIOLOGICAL PEST CONTROL
A way of controlling the populations of pests using a living **organism**. This is part of nature and does not put harmful chemicals into the soil or atmosphere.

BORAX
A naturally occurring, white crystalline compound of the chemical boron. It dissolves readily in water and can be used for a variety of cleaning purposes.

CADMIUM
A highly toxic metallic element classified, along with its compounds, as carcinogenic to humans by the IARC. Cadmium is harmful to all **organisms** and, in humans, can cause kidney failure.

CARBON DIOXIDE
An oxide of carbon, often referred to by its chemical formula CO_2. Carbon dioxide is a by-product of respiration in plants and animals. It is also released in the combustion of **fossil fuels**, ie burning carbon-rich fuels in the presence of oxygen. Carbon dioxide is a **greenhouse gas**.

CARBON NEUTRAL
Being carbon neutral means you balance the emissions of carbon dioxide you cause by removing the same amount of carbon from the atmosphere. For example you could plant trees, which take in carbon dioxide as they grow. **Biodiesel** is carbon-neutral if new crops are planted to replace those used as fuel.

CHLORINE
A yellowy-green, gaseous element, toxic by inhalation, ingestion or skin contact. Chlorine is very toxic to aquatic **organisms** once dissolved in water. Chlorine compounds are used as bleaching agents.

CHLOROFLUOROCARBONS (CFCs)
These chemicals were used as propellants in aerosols (gases used to force out the aerosols' contents) and refrigerants in fridges and freezers until it was discovered that they cause **ozone** depletion. They are largely responsible for the hole in the ozone layer. CFCs contain atoms of chlorine, which can be released by ultraviolet light in the upper atmosphere. These chlorine 'radicals' are then free to break down atmospheric ozone.

COLTAN (COLUMBITE-TANTALITE)
A metallic ore containing tantalum, which is used in capacitors (electrical devices found in computers, for example, which can hold an electrical charge).

CYANIDE
Any of a number of compounds containing the 'cyano group' (a carbon atom triple-bonded to one of nitrogen). Not all cyanides are toxic, but the sodium cyanide used to strip gold from its ore is lethal.

DESERTIFICATION
The process by which land is made unsuitable for agriculture, often due to human activity. Deforestation exposes land to the elements. Topsoil is blown from exposed fields, while overgrazing and intensive farming methods rob the land of its nutrients – effectively transforming it into barren desert.

DIOXINS
Highly toxic, **bioaccumulative** compounds produced as a by-product of some industrial processes, through waste incineration and through burning fuels. They are carcinogenic and known hormone disruptors.

ECO-LABEL
An award given by the European Union (EU) to those goods that meet certain strict criteria to minimize the environmental impact of consumer products. Eco-labelled electrical appliances, for example, are particularly energy efficient.

ENERGY SAVING RECOMMENDED LOGO

Developed by the Energy Saving Trust, this logo can be found on energy-efficient white goods (washing machines etc.), light bulbs, gas boilers and heating controls.

ENERGY STAR LOGO

This logo can be found on energy-efficient electrical equipment including computers, monitors, printers, faxes and photocopiers.

FORMALDEHYDE

A gaseous, very toxic compound classified as carcinogenic to humans by the IARC. Formaldehyde dissolves in water and is readily absorbed through the skin. It can cause damage to mucous membranes, the eyes and skin, and is known to cause genetic mutation resulting in deformities.

FOSSIL FUELS

Carbon-rich, combustible compounds formed over millions of years, including coal, **petroleum** and gas. They are the remains of pre-historic **organisms** and ancient vegetation, compressed and heated under thick layers of sediment.

GLOBAL WARMING POTENTIAL

This is a measure of the impact a gas will have on the atmosphere over the next 100 years, relative to **carbon dioxide**. For example, methane has a global warming potential of 23. This means that, averaged over the next century, a tonne of methane will have 23 times the atmospheric warming impact of a tonne of carbon dioxide.

GREENHOUSE EFFECT

Gases surrounding the Earth trap heat, warming the Earth in what is known as the greenhouse effect. The enhanced greenhouse effect, caused by the emission of large amounts of **greenhouse gases** by human activity, is causing global warming.

GREENHOUSE GAS

Any of several gases thought to contribute to the **greenhouse effect**, including **carbon dioxide**, methane, water vapour, nitrous oxide and **hydrofluorocarbons**.

GREY WATER

Slightly soiled water from the bath, kitchen sink, dishwasher or washing machine. Grey water can be reused in the home and garden – to flush toilets or water plants, for example.

HEAVY METALS

Certain metallic elements (pure metals) that are toxic to plants and animals. The term can be used in a broader sense to cover almost all the metallic elements – including those essential for good health (eg iron, copper and zinc) and the radioactive metals (eg thorium and uranium).

HYDROFLUOROCARBONS (HFCs)

A group of potent **greenhouse gases**. They each have a **global warming potential** several hundred to several thousand times that of **carbon dioxide**. Unlike **CFCs**, HFC molecules do not contain chlorine atoms and therefore do not contribute to **ozone** depletion.

LEAD

A toxic metallic element and cumulative poison in animals. Long-term exposure to lead can cause kidney disease, reproductive problems and irreversible neurological damage.

LIQUID CRYSTAL DISPLAY (LCD)

An energy-efficient electronic display device now used in computer monitors and flat televisions. Along with other flat-screen systems, it replaces the traditional method of image display using a bulky cathode-ray tube, that fires electrons at a curved fluorescent screen.

MERCURY

A highly toxic and **bioaccumulative** liquid metallic element. Mercury can be absorbed through the skin and long-term exposure is often fatal. The effects of mercury poisoning include damage to the kidneys and central nervous system. In the 19th century, hat-makers were exposed to mercury while shaping felt hats, which is where the expression 'mad as a hatter' comes from.

METHANE

The principle component of natural gas. It has 23 times the **global warming potential** of **carbon dioxide**.

NITROGEN

A gas that makes up 78 per cent of our atmosphere. As the basis of proteins, it is an important element in biological systems. Gaseous nitrogen is 'fixed' by bacteria into more complex compounds (including ammonia and nitrates). These compounds are then converted into proteins by growing plants. Ammonia and nitrate-based fertilizers are often administered to crops in order to enhance this natural process and accelerate plant growth.

NITROUS OXIDE

A gaseous compound of nitrogen and oxygen. Nitrous oxide has 296 times the **global warming potential** of **carbon dioxide**. It should not be confused with other **oxides of nitrogen** eg nitric oxide.

ORGANIC

An ecologically sound and animal-friendly farming practice. Confusingly, 'organic' can also refer to a chemical compound containing carbon (except carbon monoxide and dioxide). Thus volatile organic compounds (**VOCs**) are organic because they contain carbon atoms, not because they are environmentally friendly.

ORGANISM

An individual form of life, such as a plant, animal, fungus or a tiny bacterium.

OXIDE OF NITROGEN

Any of the group of compounds containing only oxygen and nitrogen atoms. When released into the upper atmosphere, by supersonic aircraft for example, the oxides of nitrogen break down atmospheric **ozone**.

OZONE

Ozone gas is a toxic combination of oxygen atoms that occurs naturally in the upper atmosphere from a height of about 14 kilometres. There it forms a gaseous layer, absorbing harmful ultraviolet radiation from the Sun. Ozone found near the Earth's surface is a harmful air pollutant that can cause lung problems and throat irritations.

PESTICIDE

A chemical agent applied to plants and crops to kill or deter unwanted **organisms**. Insecticides are designed to target insect pests; herbicides destroy weeds; while fungicides are used against fungal infections.

PETROCHEMICAL

A synthetic compound manufactured from **petroleum** or natural gas.

PETROLEUM

Also known as crude oil, petroleum is a mixture of hydrocarbons (combustible compounds) extracted from underground fields across the world. Petroleum is distilled in oil refineries to separate the hydrocarbons into different fuel oils including paraffin, naphtha, diesel oil, petrol and LPG. All these products, as well as the crude oil itself, are classed as **fossil fuels**.

PHOSPHATES
Naturally occurring combinations of phosphorous and oxygen. Phosphates have an important part to play in the biological processes in living **organisms**. Excessive levels of phosphates in the environment can lead to **algal blooms**.

PHOSPHOR
A material that will slowly and continuously release energy in the form of light after some initial stimulation. Phosphors are made from **heavy metals** and their compounds and are used in fluorescent lights and cathode-ray tubes.

POLYSTYRENE
A hard, brittle, colourless and transparent **petroleum**-derived plastic. Polystyrene is used in yoghurt pots, margarine tubs, vending cups and CD cases. A hydrocarbon 'expanding agent' can be added to balloon the plastic into low-density Expanded Polystyrene (EPS) – a lightweight insulating material that is often used in packaging.

POLYVINYL CHLORIDE (PVC)
A common, versatile plastic made with chlorine and often softened (plasticized) with hormone-disrupting chemicals called phthalates. **Dioxins** are released during production of the vinyl chloride molecule used as the building block for PVC, and again when the plastic is burned.

RoHS DIRECTIVE
Properly known as The Restriction of the Use of Certain Hazardous Substances in Electrical and Electronic Equipment Directive. This is a system whereby electronic equipment containing more than the agreed levels of **lead**, **cadmium** and **mercury** is prevented from entering the EU market.

SMELTING
The process whereby some metals are extracted from their ores. The ore is heated along with a source of carbon (such as coke) and a 'flux' material to remove bits of rock. The carbon reacts with any oxygen present (oxygen being the chief impurity in any metal ore) to form **carbon dioxide**, which escapes, leaving the pure, molten metal behind. Aluminium does not relinquish oxygen in quite the same way. It has to be extracted from aluminium ore (bauxite) using an electrical process known as 'industrial electrolysis'.

SYNTHETIC CHEMICAL
A human-made compound. Many naturally occurring chemicals can be reproduced synthetically and not all synthetics are toxic to the environment. The consequences of overloading an ecosystem with new (or otherwise naturally occurring) compounds are often impossible to predict and difficult to monitor. This book focuses on synthetics that are known to persist in the environment, **bioaccumulate**, and/or poison plants and animals.

TCO LABEL
A sign of energy efficiency. The TCO (Swedish Confederation of Professional Employees) label also certifies that office equipment, such as monitors, computers, furniture and mobile phones, has been produced to a set of ecological standards.

VOLATILE ORGANIC COMPOUND (VOC)
These chemicals are found in thousands of different products including certain paints, cleaning products and pesticides. They vaporize easily and enter the atmosphere. The vapours can irritate the eyes, nose and throat and cause long-term health problems. Some VOCs are carcinogenic and almost all cause ground-level ozone.

USEFUL WEBSITES

You can get more information about how to save the planet from these websites. You must get your parents' permission before you buy anything from a site.

ABOUT ORGANICS – www.aboutorganics.co.uk
A guide to everything organic, including food, clothing, skin care and gardening. Contains information, advice and links to retailers of organic products.

A&C BLACK – www.acblack.com/youcansavetheplanet
This website accompanies this book. Download copies of the diary pages, calculate your carbon footprint and share your planet-saving tips.

BIGBARN – www.bigbarn.co.uk
The BigBarn website tells you where you can get food from local producers. The site also tells you where you can find a farmers' market near you.

THE BLUE CROSS – www.bluecross.org.uk
If you are considering adopting a rescued animal, the Blue Cross website gives useful information and contact details of adoption centres.

**BORNEO ORANGUTAN SURVIVAL FOUNDATION UK
– www.savetheorangutan.org.uk**
BOS works to save orangutans and the forests they live in. Their website provides information about orangutans in Borneo and how you can help to save them.

BRITISH ASSOCIATION FOR FAIR TRADE SHOPS – www.bafts.org.uk
The British Association of Fair Trade Shops is a network of independent fairtrade shops across the UK. This site give information about Fairtrade products and where you can buy them.

CARBON FOOTPRINT – www.carbonfootprint.com
You can find out here how to calculate, reduce and offset your carbon footprint.

CLEAN SLATE – www.cleanslateclothing.co.uk
Clean Slate is a Fairtrade and organic school uniform supplier.

CLIMATE CHANGE (A BBC WEATHER CENTRE SITE)
– www.bbc.co.uk/climate
A site containing information about the evidence and impact of climate change.

COMMUNITY COMPOSTING NETWORK – www.communitycompost.org
This site gives advice on how to make compost at home.

CIWF (COMPASSION IN WORLD FARMING) – www.ciwf.org.uk
The CIWF campaigns to improve the lives of farm animals all over the world.

COOL KIDS FOR A COOL CLIMATE – www.coolkidsforacoolclimate.com
This site explains the causes and effects of climate change and tells you how you can take action to stop it.

EAT LESS MEAT – www.eatlessmeat.org
This site from CIWF provides advice on why you could consider eating less meat and what you can eat instead. There are also lots of vegetarian recipes for you and your family to try out.

ENCAMS – www.encams.org
ENCAMS is an environmental charity that campaigns against littering. Its best known campaign is 'Keep Britain Tidy'. It tackles issues such as discarded chewing gum and dog fouling. The website provides information about its campaigns and gives advice on what you can do to help and what to do if you have a particular problem near you.

ENERGY SAVING TRUST – www.energysavingtrust.org.uk
The Energy Saving Trust is a non-profit organization that was set up by the government to address the damaging effects of climate change. The website gives you information on how you can save energy at home and also gives energy-saving tips for drivers.

ENVIRONMENT IN *THE GUARDIAN* NEWSPAPER
– http://environment.guardian.co.uk
The Guardian newspaper publishes lots of articles about protecting the environment, which you can read on this website.

FAIR DEAL TRADING – www.fairdealtrading.com
A website selling Fairtrade sports balls, shoes, shirts and other sports products.

FAIRTRADE LABELLING ORGANIZATIONS INTERNATIONAL
– www.fairtrade.net
The FLO is a network of organizations around the world that promote and market the Fairtrade Certification Mark in their countries.

FOOD STANDARDS AGENCY – www.foodstandards.gov.uk
This site provides useful information on food labelling, organic food, food safety and genetically modified crops.

ENERGY STAR – www.energystar.gov
The Energy Star Program is a joint programme of the US Environmental Protection Agency and the US Department of Energy. The website provides information about products that use less energy, save money and help to protect the environment.

**THE EUROPEAN RECYCLING COMPANY LIMITED
– www.europeanrecycling.co.uk**
The European Recycling Company specializes in recycling unwanted shoes. Once collected, the shoes are sorted for suitability and distributed to developing countries.

FOREST STEWARDSHIP COUNCIL – www.fsc.org/en
The Forest Stewardship Council is an international organization that promotes responsible stewardship of the world's forests.

FRIENDS OF THE EARTH – www.foe.co.uk
Friends of the Earth campaign for solutions to environmental problems. This site provides information about their campaigns and how to get involved.

FURNITURE REUSE NETWORK – www.frn.org.uk
The Furniture Reuse Network recycle and reuse furniture and pass it on to people in need. The website will tell you how you can donate furniture to a local charity.

GREENER SOLUTIONS – www.greenersolutions.com
Use this website to sell your old mobile phone online. Greener Solutions focuses on the reuse and recycling of mobile phones and inkjet cartridges.

GREENCHOICES – www.greenchoices.org
The Green Choices website provides simple, direct information on how to have a green lifestyle with tips on lots of different topics including clothes, energy, recycling and pets.

**IFOAM (INTERNATIONAL FEDERATION OF ORGANIC AGRICULTURE
MOVEMENTS) – www.ifoam.org**
The IFOAM website provides many interesting facts and figures about organic agriculture and farming, as well as information about the world of organic agriculture.

INTERNATIONAL FAIR TRADE ASSOCIATION – www.ifat.org
The International Fair Trade Association website provides information about Fairtrade. It also lists and explains the different standards that Fairtrade organizations must follow.

LOCAL FOOD (A SOIL ASSOCIATION SITE) – www.localfoodworks.org
This is a website linked to the Soil Association. It will help you to find out where you can get locally produced food.

MAILING PREFERENCE SERVICE – www.mpsonline.org.uk
By registering with the Mailing Preference Service you can avoid junk mail and significantly reduce paper waste.

THE MOBILE PHONE RECYCLING COMPANY – www.mobilephonerecycling.co.uk

This website offers advice and contact details for recycling your old mobile phone.

NATIONAL ENERGY FOUNDATION – www.nef.org.uk

This site provides information for anyone interested in saving energy. There are factsheets about renewable energy and links to many good sites about saving energy.

ORGANICFOODEE – www.organicfoodee.com

OrganicFoodee is an online organic food magazine. It provides organic food news, organic stories, organic reviews and a free newsletter.

OXFAM – www.oxfam.org.uk

This site provides information on how to get involved in recycling. Oxfam can turn unwanted goods into cash. For example, every unwanted mobile phone donated to the 'Bring Back Scheme' is worth five pounds to Oxfam.

POLAR BEARS INTERNATIONAL – www.polarbearsinternational.org

Polar Bears International supports research projects that benefit the world's polar bears. This site provides information on polar bears and how to get involved with helping them.

RECYCLE-MORE – www.recycle-more.co.uk

This site helps you to find your nearest bottle bank or recycling centre.

RECYLEZONE – www.recyclezone.org.uk

Recyclezone is aimed at schools, children and teachers and explains what's what in the world of waste. There are games, activities and facts, as well as information on the 3Rs – Reducing, Reusing and Recycling.

RECYCLING APPEAL – www.recyclingappeal.com

The Recycling Appeal collects mobile phones and printer cartridges for reuse and recycling, raising funds and helping the environment. This site explains why recycling is important and provides information on how to get involved.

SAFEPALMOIL – http://safepalmoil.com

The Safe Palm Oil website provides information on the devastation that the palm oil industry causes to orangutan habitats in Sumatra and Borneo. It also tells you how you can help the campaign to promote safe palm oil.

SOIL ASSOCIATION – www.soilassociation.org

The Soil Association is the UK's leading environmental charity promoting sustainable and organic farming. The website gives advice on growing your own organic produce. There is also a directory of local organic groups and farms.

SOLAR ENERGY ALLIANCE – www.solarenergyalliance.com

This site offers information and advice on solar power.

SUSTRANS – www.sustrans.org.uk

Sustrans is the UK's leading sustainable transport charity. The site explains the benefits of cycling and shows you where your nearest cycle routes are.

THINK ENERGY – www.think-energy.co.uk

The Think Energy programme aims to encourage young people to be more energy efficient and to be aware of energy issues. There are many fun online activities as well as top tips for saving energy.

THE TRAVEL FOUNDATION – www.thetravelfoundation.org.uk

The Travel Foundation is a charity that promotes sustainable travel. It aims to protect the local environment that you visit and its wildlife and preserve local cultures and traditions. The website shows you how you can help.

UNIFORM2 – www.uniform2.com

Uniform2 is a free online community for buying and selling second-hand school uniform as well as books, sports equipment and musical instruments.

WASTECONNECT – www.wasteconnect.co.uk

This site helps you to find your nearest bottle bank or recycling centre. It also provides factsheets that tell you everything you need to know about recycling.

WASTE ONLINE – www.wasteonline.org.uk

Waste online provides information and facts about waste disposal in the UK. It also gives you contact details for companies that recycle computers and electrical equipment.

WATER WISE (A THAMES WATER SITE) – waterwise.fortune-cookie.com

Water Wise is committed to preserving the environment and conserving valuable water resources in the UK. The website provides information and advice on reducing water usage in the home and office.

WHYORGANIC (A SOIL ASSOCIATION SITE) – www.whyorganic.org

This site gives you nutritional advice, tips on growing your own organic vegetables, seasonal recipes and a directory of organic companies.

YOUNG LONDON TEENS – BE GREEN – www.london.gov.uk/young-london/teens/issue-zone/be-green

The site provides facts and information on climate change and pollution, rubbish and recycling and the different ways you can help the environment. There is also advice on other teen issues, such as health, food and the law.

YOUNG PEOPLE'S TRUST FOR THE ENVIRONMENT – www.yptenc.org.uk

The Young People's Trust for the Environment is a charity that aims to encourage young people's understanding of the environment and the need for sustainability. There are loads of factsheets about animals and the environment and action sheets that tell you how to make compost, paper and even a nestbox for birds.

The publishers would like to thank the following for their kind permission to reproduce their photographs:

b=bottom; c=centre; t=top; l=left; r=right

4br Anastasios Kandris/iStockphoto; **7c** Monika Wisniewska/iStockphoto; **8c** iStockphoto; **10c** Nick Free/iStockphoto; **12bl** iStockphoto; **13cr** Kenneth Chelette/iStockphoto; **14c** Daniel Bendjy/iStockphotos; **15cr** Warwick Listerkaye/iStockphoto; **16c** Derek Dammann/iStockphoto; **18c** Niels Laan/iStockphoto; **20c** iStockphoto; **22br** Alex Bramwell/iStockphoto; **24c** iStockphoto; **27tr** David Cannings-Bushell/iStockphoto;**28c** Miroslav Tolimir/iStockphoto; **30c** Andy Green/iStockphoto; **31bc** Carole Gomez/iStockphoto; **31tr** Zoran Djekic/iStockphoto; **32tc** iStockphoto; **33bc** Cole Vineyard/iStockphoto; **33c** Sally Carns/iStockphoto; **34c** Eric Naud/iStockphoto; **36c** Marcel Pelletier/iStockphoto; **38cl** Carole Gomez/iStockphoto; **39cl** James Steidl/iStockphoto; **40c** Marcelo Wain/iStockphoto; **44cl** Marc Dietrich/iStockphoto; **44tr** Gautier Willaume/iStockphoto; **45tr** Melih Kesmen/iStockphoto; **45c** Gautier Wilaume/iStockphoto; **46c** Edyta Pawtowska/iStockphoto; **48cl** iStockphoto; **49c** Tom Nance/iStockphoto; **50c** Aleksandr Ugorenkov/iStockphoto; **51bc** Qilux/iStockphoto; **52c** Suprijono Suharjoto/iStockphoto; **54bl** Holly Kuchera/iStockphoto; **55tr** Bill Grove/iStockphoto; **57c** John Sigler/iStockphoto; **58c** Jonny McCullagh/iStockphoto; **60bl** Michael Kemter/iStockphoto; **61tr** Simon Smith/iStockphoto; **62c** Sandie Howard/iStockphoto; **64c** Norman Reid/iStockphoto; **65bc** iStockphoto; **66c** iStockphoto; **68Bc** Peter Clark/iStockphoto; **69tr** iStockphoto; **70tr** Tony Campbell/iStockphoto; **70br** iStockphoto; **70c** iStockphoto; **70cl** iStockphoto; **72c** iStockphoto; **74c** Matt Craig/iStockphoto; **76c** Tammy Peluso/iStockphoto; **77bc** Joshua Blake/iStockphoto; **77tr** Dave White/iStockphoto; **78tr** Satu Knape/iStockphoto; **78c** Dan Tero/iStockphoto; **80c** Rafal Zdeb/iStockphoto; **82cl** Nick Free/iStockphoto; **83cr** Galina Barskaya/iStockphoto; **84c** Robert Gubbins/iStockphoto; **86bl** Bobbie Osbourne/iStockphoto; **87t** Christine Balderas/iStockphoto; **87cr** Matej Michelizza/iStockphoto; **88c** Susan Stewart/iStockphoto; **90c** Pali Rao/iStockphoto; **92bc** iStockphoto; **93c** Felix Alim/iStockphoto; **94c** Mageda Merbouh/iStockphoto; **95tr** Suzannah Skelton/iStockphoto; **96c** Stockphoto; **98c** Michaela Fehiker/iStockphoto; **100bl** iStockphoto; **101tr** Anna Sirotina/iStockphoto; **102c** Sean Locke/iStockphoto; **104c** iStockphoto; **104b** Stefan Tordenmalm/iStockphoto; **105tl** Edyta Pawlowska/iStockphoto; **106tr** Alice Millikan/iStockphoto; **107b** Bart broek/iStockphoto; **108c** Peter Jenson/iStockphoto; **110c** Alain Couillaud/iStockphoto; **112bl** Eric Isselee/iStockphoto; **112br** Thomas Hottner/iStockphoto; **113bc** Ira Bachinskaya/iStockphoto; **114c** Pamela Moore/iStockphoto; **116tc** Aleksandr Lobanov/iStockphoto; **117bl** iStockphoto; **118c** Jim Jurica/iStockphoto; **120bl** Ewa Walicka/iStockphoto; **121tr** Suzannah Skelton/iStockphoto; **122c** Bjorn Kindler/iStockphoto; **123cr** iStockphoto; **124cr** iStockphoto; **126c** Galina Barskaya/iStockphoto; **128cl** Liv Friis-Larsen/iStockphoto; **130c** iStockphoto; **132c** Andrey Pustovoy/iStockphoto; **133t** Richard Goerg/iStockphoto; **133bl** Viktor Kitaykin/iStockphoto; **134t** Baldur Tryggvason/iStockphoto; **134bl** Nicholas Homrich/iStockphoto; **135br** iStockphoto; **136c** Joe Carter/iStockphoto; **138c** Nick Schlax/iStockphoto; **138bl** Lisa F. Young/iStockphoto; **140c** iStockphoto; **142bc** Jan Rihak/iStockphoto; **143t** Eileen Hart/iStockphoto; **144c** Gillian Mowbray/iStockphoto; **147c** Suprijono Suharjoto/iStockphoto; **148c** Henk Jelsma/iStockphoto; **150c** Henk Jelsma/iStockphoto; **152c** Henk Jelsma/iStockphoto; **154c** Henk Jelsma/iStockphoto; **156c** Henk Jelsma/iStockphoto; **158c** Henk Jelsma/iStockphoto; **160c** Mark Strevens/iStockphoto; **167c** William Walsh/iStockphoto.

Illustrations: Jill Plank